At sunset

Julia Ward Howe

Contents

AT SUNSET

BY

Julia Ward Howe

OCCASIONAL POEMS

ABRAHAM LINCOLN

READ BY MRS. HOWE AT THE LINCOLN CENTENARY MEETING IN
SYMPHONY HALL, BOSTON, FEBRUARY 12,1909

THROUGH the dim pageant of the years
A wondrous tracery appears:
A cabin of the western wild
Shelters in sleep a new-born child.

Nor nurse, nor parent dear can know
The way those infant feet must go;
And yet a nation's help and hope
Are sealed within that horoscope.

Beyond is toil for daily bread,
And thought, to noble issues led,
And courage, arming for the morn
For whose behest this man was born.

A man of homely, rustic ways,
Yet he achieves the forum's praise,
And soon earth's highest meed has won,
The seat and sway of Washington.

No throne of honors and delights;
Distrustful days and sleepless nights,
To struggle, suffer, and aspire,
Like Israel, led by cloud and fire.

A treacherous shot, a sob of rest,
A martyr's palm upon his breast,
A welcome from the glorious seat
Where blameless souls of heroes meet;

And, thrilling through unmeasured days,
A song of gratitude and praise;
A cry that all the earth shall heed,
To God, who gave him for our need.

FULTON

READ BY MRS. HOWE AT THE HUDSON-FULTON CELEBRATION IN
NEW YORK, SEPTEMBER, 1909

A RIVER flashing like a gem,
Crowned with a mountain diadem,
Invites an unaccustomed guest
To launch his shallop on her crest —
A pilgrim whose exploring mind
Must leave his tardy pace behind:
"My bark creeps slow, the world is vast,
How shall its space be overpassed? "

Responsive to his cry appears
A visionary, young in years,

Commissioned with prophetic brain
The mystic problem to explain:
"Where fire and water closest blend,
There find a servant and a friend!"

Yet many a moon must wax and wane,
With sleepless nights and days of pain,
Pleadings a monarch's court before,
Shrewd processes and study sore,
Ere on the silver tide shall float,
Swifter than thought, young Fulton's boat.

And not alone for Hudson's stream
Avails the magic power of steam.
Blessings of unimagined worth
Its speed shall carry round the earth;
Knowledge shall on its pinions fly,
Nor land nor race in darkness lie;

Commerce her hoards shall freely bring
To many an urgent summoning,
And Want and Wealth, in sundered lands,
Shall closely clasp redeeming hands,
While master minds new gospels span,
The holy brotherhood of Man.

Rest, Fulton, in thine honored grave,
Remembered with the wise and brave.
Not wholly dost thou yield to death,
For on the wind blows fiery breath,
And on the wave the solemn tread
Of multitudes o'er ocean led,
And in our grateful hearts a shrine

Of loving memory, all are thine.

And as one sun doth compass all
That can arise, or may befall;
One sentence on Creation's night
Bestowed the blessed boon of light,
So shall all life one promise fill
Of gentle nurture and good will,
While, pledge of Love's assured control,
The Flag of Freedom crowns the pole.

THE CAPITOL

FOR THE FIRST MEETING OF THE AMERICAN ACADEMY OF ARTS
AND LETTERS, WASHINGTON, DECEMBER 14-16, 1900

WHERE shall our nation's temple stand ?
Centre of counsel and command;
A Mecca of unfailing faith;
A Zion of unwavering hope;
A fortress that with grim assault
And deadly stratagem may cope;
A Rome that weaves no slavish bond,
But wins allegiance firm and fond.

I see the noble structure rise,
The dome descending from the skies
To lofty station, that the eye
And will of man may aim so high,
While walls of hospitable space
The people's judgment-seat embrace.
Here shall avail the argument

Of just endeavor and intent;
Here shall the widow's prayer be brought,
The orphan's sacred claim be sought;
The heavenly sisterhood of art
Keeping unstained a nation's heart;

An altar for each honest creed,
A court where each just cause may plead,
A sentence of eternal lore
Uttered in whispers heretofore,
But now with silver trump proclaimed
To men and regions newly named,
That right with right may fitly join,
The weal of each for all combine;
No need to snatch, no need to slay,
For a republic's holiday.
The chief who gave our shrine his name
Barred it thenceforth from evil fame.
Upon his laureled tomb doth lie
The pledge of immortality,
For all his way was writ of Fate
In holy footsteps consecrate.

Where the sad spoils of warfare rest
Nirvana sits, a solemn guest,
Safeguard of rule that may not cease,
Sponsor of righteousness and peace.

How shall we overmatch the past
With merits, shaming each the last ?
Fast holding each illustrious theft
Old Time has patterned in his weft,
Losing no touch of hero song,

Yielding no step of vanquished wrong,

No conquering grace that marks the line
Where human beauties grow divine.
Let him who stands for service here
With deeply reverent soul draw near,
Intent from every season's youth
To pluck the new commissioned truth;
To lift the weight that most offends,
The need that other needs transcends;
In distant prisons, sad and drear,
The captive's lonely heart to cheer,
And in earth's wildest wastes arouse
The music of the Father's house —
Home for the homeless, priceless rest,
Heaven's seal of promise, dearest, best.

THE MARINER'S DREAM

READ AT CENTRAL PARK AT THE UNVEILING OF THE COLUMBUS STATUE, MAY 12, 1894

WHERE shall we find the golden key
That opes to peace and liberty?
The earth is full of grievous wars,
The soldier's tread her beauty mars,
The captive's chains are fast and locked,
The poor man by the rich man mocked.
The promise of the Christ we hear,
But who shall bring fulfillment near?

A dream came to a sailor bold,

A happy dream of good untold;
And a little bird sang: "Follow me
Westward, over the unknown sea.
A star shall lead thy chosen band,
And bring thy slender craft to land.
Beyond the waters thou shalt find
Regions of splendor unconfined,
Where giant rivers fruitful flow,
Where birds of tropic plumage glow,
Where the old treasures of thy race
Shall grow and multiply apace.

And ancient Rule renew its health
In a new glorious commonwealth."

The dreamer waking, bowed his head,
And on the wondrous errand sped.
With pleading rare he wrung the gold
From hands reluctant to unfold,
And loosing from old Europe's shore
Sailed westward, westward evermore.

"I hear a whisper in the breeze,
Whispered from forests of strange trees,
From depths of greenery unexplored,
Where sounded ne'er the Christian word.
I may not feed on light-earned bread,
Nor on soft pillow rest my head,
For still my wandering thoughts obey
The mystic voice that calls away.

"What though the way be long to find,
Traced dimly in my laboring mind;

Though wild impatience seize my crew,
Distrustful of the venture new;
Should all mankind against me turn,
The haven gained, my wage shall earn,
The yet undowered Future claim
Earth's noblest conquest in my name."

Oh, man of visions, sorely vexed!
Denied, deserted, and perplexed;
Shamed by rebuke from royal lips,
And Fame and Fortune's sad eclipse,
Thy furrow traced across the sea
The unseen path of destiny.
In thy firm hand the steadfast helm
Steered onward to the magic realm.
And now from out the centuries' maze
Millions of voices sing thy praise,
And hail those conquering footsteps trod,
Inspired of angels, led by God.

Here gather we in Gotham town,
Of all our western world the crown,
While ladies fair and gallants gay
Unite to celebrate the day.
But while we list the high discourse,
And while the Paean has its course,
Let Faith re-consecrate this form,
Adventured once 'gainst sea and storm.

For 't was this hand that held the key,
Unlocking Peace and Liberty.
When all we have and all we are
Hung on the guidance of a star,

And on the answer, dimly guessed
In one resolved, responsive breast.

NEW YORK

SHE sits beside the ocean,
With a river on either hand,
And all the wealth of waters
By giant girdles spanned.

Like messengers of gladness
The swift sails come and go,
Full-freighted with a promise
The hungry world should know,

Since to Earth's farthest limits
They bear the precious spoil
Wrung from the gold-paved caverns,
Brought from the teeming soil.

Voices of many nations
Make music in the streets,
Their blooded pulses quicken
The heart that steadfast beats.

Brave blood she brought from
Britain, From Holland careful thrift,
And ancient empires taught her
Their wisdom and uplift.

She yields to helpful labor
Its meed and honor fit,
And in her princely mansions

The peasant's son may sit.

God grant our noble city
Forever thus to stand,
A sentinel of freedom,
Guarding a blessed land.

February 14,1902.

OLD HOME WEEK IN BOSTON

ROME, on her hills of vantage throned,
Gave to the world her strenuous rule.
Isles of the sea her empire owned,
The Nations studied at her school.

Resplendent from her gates went forth
The legions of her proud defence,
And fiery South and frozen North
Did homage to her eminence.

Heroic souls her counsels gave;
Wisdom her sturdy conquests held;
Her towering eagle, fierce and brave,
The tumult of the peoples quelled.

The forest broods a better way
Than the rude clutch of Rapine saw.
Within her walls, to stand for aye,
Was crowned the majesty of Law.

Our City is as nobly set,
Stately her hills, albeit but three, Glorious about her parapet

Floats the dear Flag of Liberty.

Strong sons, the nurslings of her hearth,
For freedom won the Western plains;
To-day, with happy pride of birth,
They come to show their splendid gains.

Fair towns they builded as they went;
Empires above their footsteps grew;
For Justice stood their armament,
For all th' illustrious truth they knew,
Now, welcome young and welcome old!
Salute with joy each sacred bound!
The cradle of your race behold!
Let the ancestral anthems sound!
And let our Boston, from her heights,
Match with her hills the virtues three,
And crown them, as with beacons bright,
With Faith and Hope and Charity.

LEXINGTON CENTENNIAL

APRIL 19TH, 1875

ONE hundred years the world hath seen,
Since, bristling on these meadows green,
The British foeman mocked our sires,
New armed beside their household fires.

The troops were hastening from the town
To hold the country for the Crown;
But through the land the ready thrill
Of patriot hearts ran swifter still.

Our Fathers met at break of dawn.
From many a peaceful haunt they come;
From homely task and rustic care,
Marshalled by faith, upheld by prayer.

The winter's wheat was in the ground,
Waiting the April zephyr's sound;
But other growth these fields should bear
When War's wild summons rent the air.

Here flowed the sacrificial blood,
Hence sprang the bond of Brotherhood;
Here rose resolved for good or ill,
The Nation's majesty of will.

Oh Thou who Victor dost remain
Above the slayer and the slain,
Not ill we deem that in Thy might,
That day, our fathers held their right.

They knew not that their ransomed land
To free the vassal'd Earth should stand;
That Thou, through all their toil and pain,
A home of nations didst ordain.

Upon this field of Lexington
We hail the mighty conquest won,
Invoking here Thy mightier name
To keep our heritage from shame,

May peaceful generations turn
To where these ancient glories burn;

And not a lesson of that time
Fade from men's thoughts through wrong and crime.

Beside the hearth let freemen still
Keep their integrity of will,
And meet the treason of the hour
With mind resolved and steadfast power.

But not in arms be our defence;
Give us the strength of innocence,
The will to work, the heart to dare
For Truth's great battle, everywhere.

So may ancestral conquests live
In what we have and what we give;
And the great boons we hold from
Thee Turn to enrich humanity.

A WORD FOR THE MOMENT

THE BOXER REBELLION

I

ART-ANGEL Guido hangs upon my wall
A moving picture of the Tempter's fall.
Michael, bright champion of the heavenly host,
Treads under foot the leader of the lost.

Buskined with light, with faultless weapon armed,
He stands above the prostrate foe, unharmed.
The groveling wretch no counter-blow essays,

Pinned down to earth, in impotent amaze.

This vision, oft encountered, seems to say:
The brute on earth shall never more hold sway;
While, glorious as a seraph from the skies,
Freedom makes good her deathless victories.

II

The legendary fight grows pale
Before me, as I hear the wail
Of men on noble errand sent
And held with murderous intent,
By frantic legions that essay
To stifle Europe in Cathay.

My fancy shows each pallid face,
True lovers, locked in last embrace;
Parents who to their bosoms strain
The babes they guard, but guard in vain.

And as I kneel in prayer, I cry:
Father! send rescue from on high!
The ways of human help are barred;
Be thou, O Lord! their watch and ward !

Alas! alas! their doom is sealed!
No source of succor is revealed.
But still, beyond the bounds of sense,
Prevaileth God's omnipotence.

His seraph messenger may come,

E'en to that fiend-beleaguered home,
And unto those who perish give
A crown denied to those that live.

Ruler of all! to each brave heart
The joy of martyrdom impart!
Upon thy scroll of deathless fame
Write them with those who overcame;

Who, folded in the blessed light
Of Christian faith and Christian right,
Unto the bitter end abode,
Sealed in the armory of God. 1900.

VERSES READ AT THE COOPERS-TOWN CENTENNIAL

WHAT village of the western wild
Lifts its far challenge of romance
From forests by the axe unspoiled,
From where the skin-clad sachems dance?

Whose was the note? A bard of old
Held nature subject to his song,
Whose ringing strophes, clear and bold,
The echoes of the world prolong.

So, kindled with poetic fire,
Aspiring from the virgin sod
Came he who, to our heart's desire,
The measure of the Muses trod.

What voice like his the legend taught,
The story of our pilgrim days?
The march with deadly danger fraught,
The heroes ignorant of praise:

The hunter bold, the savage dark,
The breath of regions unprofaned,
The rover with his phantom bark,
The valiant spirits, rudely trained?

Be dear to us this sylvan ground
That holds his ashes in its breast,
While songs of love and praise resound
Above the beauty of his rest,

August, 1907.

HYMN FOR THE INTERNATIONAL CONGRESS OF RELIGIOUS LIBERALS HELD IN BOSTON, 1907

HAIL! Mount of God, whereon with reverent feet
The messengers of many nations meet;
Diverse in feature, argument, and creed,
One in their errand, brothers in their need.

Not in unwisdom are the limits drawn
That give far lands opposing dusk and dawn;
One sun makes bright the all-pervading air,
One fostering spirit hovers everywhere.

So with one breath may fervent souls aspire,

With one high purpose wait the answering fire.
Be this the prayer that other prayers controls, —
That light divine may visit human souls.

The worm that clothes the monarch spins no flaw,
The coral builder works by heavenly law;
Who would to Conscience rear a temple pure
Must prove each stone and seal it, sound and sure.

Upon one steadfast base of truth we stand,
Love lifts her sheltering walls on either hand;
Arched o'er our head is Hope's transcendent dome,
And in the Father's heart of hearts our home.

SING us a song of the grand old time,
Of John Brown, martyr, our pioneer.
Tell how, in view of a nation's crime,
We breasted the wilderness, lone and drear.
Bible and rifle in hand we went,
To rear in the desert our flag and tent.

For a wicked bugle note had called
The men who would hold their fellow slave;
When, at its falseness unappalled,
Came forth a company clean and brave,
Unfettered by customs old and ill,
With the freeman's mind and the freeman's will.

Some who started in manhood's bloom
Short time abode and never returned,
But most of us stayed as we found room,
And fairly the Pilgrim's guerdon earned.
With nights of watching and days of toil,

We saved from dishonor a virgin soil.

Firm on our shoulder the Duties sate
That grow with the growth of human kind,
No worship of Fortune, nor creed of Fate,
But the leadership of the well-taught mind.
Where the wild man left but briar and thorn,
We planted the field, and gathered the corn.

And so, we builded our cities fair,
For our fathers' tongue and our fathers' faith.
The church spire hallowed our place of prayer,
The school bell uttered its blessed breath,
And he who crosses our bound shall find
That he leaves no gain of the age behind.

With many a weary task 't was done,
With murder lurking in thicket and grove,
With backs that ached 'neath a burning sun,
With homes that sheltered but thrift and love.
We lightened our labor with speech and song,
And the women worked with us, right along!

Now, half a hundred years have sped
To make the desert a blooming state;
We thank our God for honest bread,
For duteous children and loving mate,
But most, that the Fathers went out to see
The land redeemed for liberty.

THE PLAYHOUSE

READ AT THE CASTLE SQUARE THEATRE, MAY 10, 1905

'T is writ that Troy's wild prophetess
In vision mystical could guess,
When to th' Atrides roof she came,
The story of its deeds of shame —
Before her passed the victims slain,
Glowed at her feet the bloody stain.

But I, approaching this fair scene,
Divine the Joy that here hath been,
Where, each in his enchanted seat,
The lovers of the drama meet, While
Art unfolds the magic page
That charms mankind from age to age.

Here have you read in pictures fair
The lesson of the things that were;
Othello, terrible and brave,
Hamlet, discoursing o'er a grave,
Macbeth with fatal aim pursuing
The deed that ends in his undoing,
And types more modern, strange and rich,
Framed to bewilder and bewitch.

And here for countless days to come,
Shall harmless Pleasure make her home.
Here shall you mark the season's flight
With memories of pure delight, While
Wisdom in each quaint disguise

Your deeper thought shall recognise.
Your plaudits shall the Right uphold,
Your censure shame the villain bold,
Your love enthrone life's greatest good,
The glory of true humanhood.

THE NATION'S HOLIDAY

OUR fathers met in grief and gloom,
And as the Tyrant spoke their doom
They answered, " Freedom shall have room."

Backward, as to a golden store,
They looked to valiant hearts of yore,
Whose might the people's cause up-bore.

And forward, in the skies above,
They saw a heavenly banner move,
Whose virtue they were bound to prove.

For them the Galilean taught
The truth with new deliverance fraught,
And 'neath His martyr flag they fought.

Now as our world stands at a loss,
With all its treasures, all its dross
To match the riches of the Cross,

So, pomp of flags and marches gay
And martial muster and array
Are all too poor to praise this day.

How should we thank for boon so high?

How keep above the things that die
Our holy gift of Liberty?

With duteous heart revere the Past,
Its doctrine and its deeds hold fast,
But know, they should be over-passed.

The harvest that 't is ours to reap
With blood of heroes sown so deep,
A bloodless vigilance shall keep.

Build nobler temples, and enshrine
On the heart's altar pure and fine,
The Brotherhood that is divine.

For our defence throughout the land
The school with open door shall stand,
With truth and love in high command.

From us, who meet with one intent,
On due commemoration bent,
Be this fair greeting world-wide sent:

Not for us only did befall
The good we conquered; hear us call
"One freedom and one God for all!"

HYMN FOR THE FOURTH OF JULY

OUR fathers built the house of God;
Rough-hewn, with haste its slabs they laid,
The savage man in ambush trod,
And still they worshiped undismayed.

They wrought like stalwart men of war,
Who wrung the state from heathen hands;
Who bore their faith's high banner far,
And in its name possessed the lands.

The skill of strife to peaceful arts,
Their perils over, glad gave way;
The bond of freedom joined men's hearts
More near than meaner compact may.

We, followers of their task and toil,
Inherited their dangers too;
Drove bloody rapine from our soil,
Th' oppressor dared, the murderer slew.

Our heavy work, like theirs, at end;
Returning from the death-won field,
Brother with brother, friend with friend
Again the house of God we build.

Oh! may our ransomed freedom dwell
In truth's own citadel secure;
And blameless guardians foster well
The mystic flame that must endure.

The flame of holy human love,
That makes our liberties divine;
Let each strong arm its champion prove,
And each true heart its deathless shrine.
1865.

THE GLORIOUS FOURTH

UNFURL the flag, ye veterans all,
Respond to the familiar call!
Let Drum and Fife awakened be
For Freedom's glorious Reveillé !

The gathering crowds with haste obey
The joyful summons of the day.
The cannon's rhythmic boom resounds,
The snapping fire toy goes its rounds.

Above the noise, above the sport,
Shall Justice hold her sober court:
"You, people whom this day set free,
What shall you do for liberty ?"

"Our friendly harbors open stand,
To hail the ships of every land.
The fainting exile at our door
Finds cheer and welcome evermore.

With the great boon that we have gained
A holy promise is enchained.
Not for ourselves alone we fought,
But for a wide deliverance wrought.

Freedom is in the dauntless heart,
The will t' enact a noble part,
The faith that reads with reverent eyes
A message writ beyond the skies.

While yet on earth one Tyrant wields
The scourge that strips the fertile fields,
While one his iron rule doth fling
O'er men who call their conscience King,
While Right from armed Might must flee,
We are not free, we are not free.

Where sets the Autocrat his seal,
And starving hinds his prowess feel,
Where bleeds the Christian for his cross,
There do we suffer pain and loss.

As in one temple let us kneel
To pray for every nation's weal;
Then speed the messengers of peace
To cry: "The reign of blood must cease."

THE CHRISTMAS TRUCE

BETWEEN THE BRITISH AND THE BOER ARMIES DECEMBER 25, 1899

AT early dawn, one wintry day,
Two armies, oft encountering, lay
Pledged to a fierce and fatal fight,
Each hateful in the other's sight.

Why sounds no more the iron rain
Of missiles, nor the cry of pain?
And why do foemen greeting send
As to a brother, or a friend?

In ancient times of bloody war
Stood portents in the heavens afar,

And cloud-built hosts with seeming rage
Approached each other to engage.

What stood between the foes that day
To keep the battle-fiend away?
What emblem consecrates the morn?
The vision of a Babe new-born,

Foreseen in many a prophet's mind
As the Redeemer of Mankind;
Belov'd, for help that He should bring
To human woe and suffering.

The centuries that lie between
His sacred glory cannot screen.
He bids the bitter conflict cease,
And lifts His infant voice for peace.

Oh! Babe adored! What passions wild
Are stilled before that little
Child Whose gentle Mother shall become
The guardian spirit of the home!

His two small hands are stretched in love
The sanguinary fields above.
"Oh! harm each other not! " He cries.
"Henceforth encounter brotherwise."

Thus He who lived and died for all
Announced His holy festival,
And so th' opposing armies lay
At peace on blessed Christmas Day.

THE MESSAGE OF PEACE

WRITTEN FOR CHILDREN

BID the din of battle cease!
Folded be the wings of fire!
Let your courage conquer peace,—
Every gentle heart's desire.

Let the crimson flood retreat!
Blended in the arc of love,
Let the flags of nations meet;
Bind the raven, loose the dove.

At the altar that we raise
King and Kaiser may bow down;
Warrior-knights above their bays
Wear the sacred olive crown.

Blinding passion is subdued,
Men discern their common birth,
God hath made of kindred blood
All the peoples of the earth.

High and holy are the gifts
He has lavished on the race, —
Hope that quickens, prayer that lifts,
Honor's meed, and beauty's grace.

As in Heaven's bright face we look
Let our kindling souls expand;
Let us pledge, on nature's book,
Heart to heart and hand to hand.

For the glory that we saw
In the battle-flag unfurled,
Let us read Christ's better law:
Fellowship for all the world!
1899.

AFTER THE CONVENTION[1]

SOFT I hear the church bell tolling in the distance
clear and warm,
Standing thought-bound in the hollow of my little
Portsmouth farm. I to church would not be going, here is church
enough for me, Let my ducks and geese give sermon and my brook
make symphony.

What, profane one ? art thou turning from the altar, from the creed?
Can the trees impress thy conscience and the bushes help thy need?
Oh! I come from days of talking, full of reasons long drawn out.
Now, God's minister of silence comes to compass
me about.

My remembrance of the women! from the forehead crowned in white
Through the shadows brown and chestnut, to youth's tingling bloom and light;

And the thoughtful words they uttered, bright with fancy, fond with faith,
Firm with sober sense and resting upon truths that
conquer death.

But not alien to that meeting is this cluster of my trees,
Where I pick the fallen apple and attend the rustling breeze;

---

1   Evidently written many years ago, and never revised.

And the nuts are not yet gathered. Oh! the boys have need of them,
Feast thou only on the mirror pond and dazzling diadem!

They are praying as they stand there, not in doubt and not in fear,
Winter showing in the distance that shall make their beauty drear;
They endure with stern composure all the shifting of the sun,
Sighing oft the woman's whisper — let the will of God be done!

No! an impulse stolen from summer lights them up before mine eyes
As its lovely Indian changeling wafts a thought of Paradise.
In the change of things diurnal they discern the changeless law,
And great life's eternal gospel thrills their heart with sudden awe.

For that mighty truth gives freedom, far beyond the buds of spring,
And the swelling fruit of summer, and the autumn's gathering.
To the parent soul unswerving all things bud and blossom on,
And the summer's good departs not when the summer's breath is gone.

So the maple flushes fervent, looking up to Heaven's blue ken,
So the purple ash beside her breathes its soberer Amen.
And the yellow oaks in copses, with a logic of their own,
Link the litany of autumn in a mellow monotone.

Days may perish, life endureth — in the winter harsh and rude
May decline our outward beauty, not our inner power and word,
Spring shall bring us new rejoicing, autumn crown us where we stand,

When our cycles shall be numbered, still our seed shall keep the land.

What the autumn trees can pray for? What the elder women say;
Straight from Thee our being cometh, Thou who livest now and aye.
Let us hold the precious essence, like pure vases void of blame,

Handing down its sweet conditions to the things that keep our name.

But the law of life is progress; as the forests bloom and grow,
So the fortunes of great womankind in onward sweep we know.
Grant us faith to gifts imparted in the viewing of the sun,
Faithful fruitage, true transmission, and the will of God is done!

THE QUEEN'S JUBILEE

TH' assembled crowd of subjects wait
The passing of a car of state
With mounted guard and herald quaint,
With ermined peer and mitred saint.

Right royally the coursers prance,
The sovereign, glittering to the glance
With priceless gems of every clime,
Moves on with bell and trumpet chime.

Why does the splendid pageant stand
Arrested by a waving hand ?
An antic steed with murderous feet
O'erthrows an urchin of the street.

The Empress of as proud a realm
As e'er saw statesman at its helm,
Commands the pause, that she may know
What harm o'ertook that stripling low.

Where dwells the grace that fits a queen ?
In bearing haughty or serene ?
In lofty attitude of mind?
In pomps that dazzle humankind?

The queenliest action of that day
When cheering thousands marked her way,
Was that which showed how simply good
Was the great lady's womanhood.

1897.

DECORATION DAY

EARTH from her winter slumber breaks;

The morning of the year awakes.
The vital warmth that buried lay
Transcends again its house of clay,
And to the greeting of the skies
With thrilling harmony replies.

A promise breathes from every furrow:
"Dark yesterday makes bright to-morrow.
Pursue no more the midnight oil;
The sunlight measures cheer and toil;
The winds proclaim, with odorous breath,
The life that triumphs over death."

Yet vanished days of many a year
Remain to us possessions dear;
We call the roll of those who dared;
We bless the saints who hardly fared,
Lending their martyred flesh to be
The torchlight of Truth's victory.

Still may we utter solemn praise

Of those whose prowess filled their days
With thoughts and deeds of high renown,
Which now our floral offerings crown.
But as our earth from south to north
Her glorious promise blazons forth,
And timid spring and summer bold
On autumn pour their wealth of gold,

So let our buried heroes live
In hands that freely guard and give,
In minds that, watchful, entertain
Great thoughts of Justice and her reign,
That tend, all other tasks above,
The household fires of faith and love,
And keep our banner, wide unfurled,
A pledge of blessing to the world. 1908.

SCHOOL AT WELLESLEY HILLS

SAD festival, thy name recalls
The faces pictured on our walls,
The valiant hearts that many a year
Are wanting to the household cheer.

A shape went forth on bounding foot,
Returned, a prisoner dread and mute;
The blood that in its veins did leap
Stained the pale marble of its sleep.

Tears followed on those days of doom,
And garlands for the hero's tomb;
That fount of grief has never dried,
Those garlands never are denied.

Of years a score have nearly passed
Since our war bugle blew its last.
Where steel met steel for bitter loss,
The threads of reconcilement cross.

The brothers who were sundered then
The bond of kindred own again.
And South and North, and East and West,
One life thrills in one nation's breast.

Forever blessed be their name,
Forever sacred be their claim
Who fought for that heroic tie,
Who fell for Freedom's family.

Fair maids who here secluded wait
On Duty throned in Training's state,
This day to you a lesson bears
More weighty than the schoolroom's cares.

Yours is the motherhood of men,
The priesthood of life's deepened ken.
Oh! may all words of sages rise,
All poets' songs of many skies,
Teach you a wisdom deep and true,
A virtue brave, a music new.

To you Columbia fondly looks.
Informed with diagrams and books,
She sees you, steadfast, climb the hill,
Your urns from silvery fountains fill,

And, linking soft a silken band,
She lays the clasp within your hand,
And says: "Your task must never cease;
Aid noble men to keep God's peace."

THE DEPARTING CENTURY[2]

I WAS baptized in blood, and saw the light
When wrong paraded in the garb of right,
When dreams of poet and of ancient sage,
Illumining the world's confusèd page,
Were crossed with sanguine horror, guilt whose shame
Did blot the nobler with the baser name.
War's furious pulses coursed within my veins
While dear my spirit held enfranchised plains
Where heavenly peace, whom savage discords wound,
'Twixt plant and plough a refuge calm had found.

In sooth no common destiny was mine,
Truth's oracles my wisdom did divine.
Life's faded flag, in heroes' heart's blood dyed,
I raised and floated, ever to abide
Where cloud nor mist nor armament should hide.

The mellow beauty of my afternoon
Provoked the prophet's word, the poet's rune,

And sun did never set so grand and free
As mine, in gold and crimson blazonry.

---

2 Copied Oct. 14th, 1901. All this rushed into my mind one afternoon when I lay down to take my half-hour's rest. This I was forced to abbreviate in order to record the lines above. They are very rough. I wish I could improve them.

Above my ashes do not celebrate
The contests blind of old imagined
Fate. Build me enduring monuments of stone,
But no uncertain message write thereon.
Conceived in Doubt, engendered of Despair,
Pledged to all deeds that men may dream and dare,
I moved unfaltering to the solemn height
Where waning rainbows meet in perfect light.
Truth was my guest, belief in her my power,
And of such good transcendent was my dower
That I shall live in memory and in Fame
As long as man his manhood's meed may claim;
Beloved for fetters loosed, for veils unbound,
For God's great word, by God's great order crowned.

PERSONAL POEMS TO OLIVER WENDELL HOLMES

ON THE COMPLETION 07 HIS SEVENTIETH YEAR

Thou metamorphic god!
Who mak'st the steep
Olympus thy abode,
Hermes to subtle laughter moving,
Apollo with serener loving.
Thou demigod also!
Who dost all the powers of healing know;
Thou hero who dost wield
The golden sword and shield, —
Shield of a comprehensive mind,
And sword to wound the foes of human kind;

Thou man of noble mould!
Whose metal grows not cold
Beneath the hammer of the hurrying years;
A fiery breath doth blow
Across its fervid glow,
And still its resonance delights our ears.
Loved of thy brilliant mates,
Relinquished to the fates,
Whose spirit music used to chime with thine,
Transfigured in our sight,
Not quenched in death's dark night,
They hold thee in companionship divine.

Oautocratic muse!
Soul-rainbow of all hues,
Packed full of service are thy bygone years;
Thy wingfèd steed doth fly
Across the starry sky,
Bearing the lowly burthens of thy tears.

I try this little leap,
Wishing that from the deep
I might some pearl of song adventurous bring.
Despairing, here I stop —
And my poor offering drop;
Why stammer I when thou art here to sing?
1879.

OLIVER WENDELL HOLMES

How shall the Muse of vanished years
Fitly inscribe his two-fold page?
Wizard of laughter and of tears,

A master jester, and a sage.

A presence answering to the cry,
"Lord! who shall show us any good?"
A sheaf of sunbeams passing by,
In jewels of delight renewed.

Deftly he blew the pipes of Pan,
Or swept Apollo's golden lyre;
Rehearsing all the fate of Man,
How he must suffer, how aspire.

Oh! stay with us! Life cannot fail
When thou its varied values showest!
Or leave us thine immortal scale,
And all the wondrous lore thou knowest!

Weeping, we laid his form in earth,
A soldier, fallen in the trenches,
A wingfèd spirit, free of birth;
Look up! he's singing in the branches.
1894.

WASHINGTON ALLSTON

READ AT THE ALLSTON CELEBRATION 07 THE NEW ENGLAND
WOMEN'S CLUB

PRELUDE

IMMORTAL Presence of the Beautiful!
Thee our attempted festivals invoke.

In Nature's chaos, passionless and dull,
Thy voice the spell of dark disorder broke.

Ev'n as thy fiat sowed the heavens with light,
Herald of glories — torch of worlds unknown,
Souls didst thou kindle, whose effulgent light
The lustre of thy rolling orbs outshone.

Our human hearts alternate day and night,
Hopes dawn, attain their noontide, and decline;
But when their flattering sun has spent his light,
From purple depths the steadfast spirits shine.

And we who thank for breath, and health, and sense,
Our great world-sphere, its beauties and its laws,
Bless most that ministry of life intense
Whose holy office knows nor rest nor pause.

We, whispering women, like an insect band
Chirping the vespers of the summer day,
Call with our simple music, poorly planned,
On a majestic soul, beloved for aye.

RECITAL

The Puritan was strict and lone.
He set his face, like flinty stone,
His will resolved and sturdy hand
To drive the demons from the land.

In his belief, the harmful Powers
That haunt this universe of ours
Had settled purpose, form, and face,

That ever warred with saintly grace.

The shots he aimed were good and true;
A thousand evil things they slew,
Yet other evil, springing still,
Brought torment to his manly will.

"Here Law and Logic rule," he said,
"Yet Disbelief erects her head.
Sin grows apace, we work with pain,
The native demons still remain."

A whisper from the upper air
Lightened with love that heavy care,
And bade on helpful errand start
TV anointed chivalry of Art.

Supreme in that inspired band
Did Allston's genius bless the land,
Enthroning o'er the dark abyss
Transcendent forms of heavenly bliss.

Time flies away, with joys and pains;
His guardian presence still remains,
His noble fire, unquenched of death,
His sentence, passing human breath.

Those silvery curls, those lustrous eyes,
That deep regard, so kind and wise,
The habit quaint, the kindling smile
Seen in our frigid streets erewhile.

All these are lost, but not the dreams

With which his varied canvas gleams,
We lose not, with life's fleeting span,
The measure of the perfect man.

With reverence, on the tinted walls
That bear his trace, the sunlight falls;
The women that his fancy framed
Are never doubted, never shamed.

Where sits the wanton at his feast,
The Prophet's warning heeding least,
Recalling thee, his heart shall tell
How wild Belshazzar reigned, and fell.

Trimountain, crown the Master's grave!
Cherish the wondrous gifts he gave
Who, called to other spheres away
Bids yet his steadfast angels stay.

ROBERT E. LEE

READ AT THE RICHMOND CELEBRATION 07 THE HUNDREDTH AN-NIVERSARY OF GENERAL LEE'S BIRTH

A GALLANT foeman in the fight,
A brother when the fight was o'er,
The hand that led the host with might
The blessed torch of learning bore.

No shriek of shell nor roll of drums,
No challenge fierce, resounding far,
When reconciling Wisdom comes

To heal the cruel wounds of war.

Thought may the minds of men divide,
Love makes the hearts of nations one;
And so, thy soldier grave beside,
We honor thee, Virginia's son.
January 19,1907.

WILLIAM ELLERY CHANNING

WRITTEN FOR THE CENTENNIAL CELEBRATION OF HIS BIRTH, AT
NEWPORT, R. L

I COME to-day a verse to build
Which skill should match with arches fine,
A task to set the workman's guild
Whose strength shall stand for things divine.

In this fair isle, by Nature blest,
Where men for health and pleasure throng,
I call a spirit from its rest,
I summon back a soul with song.

For God who gave this genial sky,
The rapture of this mellow air,
Did lend in happy days gone by
A presence grand, an influence rare.

Our beauteous seasons wax and wane,
And bear us on to fate and death;
But he shall bloom and bloom again
In every generation's breath.

Oh! fine and brave that subtle hand
Which found the knots, so small and strong,
By which belief and passion band
To do divine and human wrong.

He caught the echo of the wail
Which once from Calvary's mountain rolled,
When felt the Love that cannot fail The
spite of superstition old.

His voice took up the trumpet blast
Which Hope's glad resurrection blew,
When out of mystic shadow passed
The glory that the Master knew.

Oh! deep of heart, oh! true of thought!
The temper of thy perfect steel
In Heaven's high armory was wrought,
The strength of Justice to reveal.

The Negro in the Southern wild
Had cause to bless thy champion name;
The Northern freeman for his child
Thy gracious heritage doth claim.

The faith that maketh Woman free
For humankind to do and dare,
The peace that dwells with liberty
Was in thy teaching and thy prayer.

Here the foundation stone we lay
Of some fine fabric that shall rise

To image to a later day
Thee, greatly good, and purely wise.

When God vouchsafes his greatest gift,
The Prophet, crown of all desire,
Let us our duteous emblem lift,
Let us endeavor and aspire.

So shall the work we strive to rear
Be crowned with blessing in our sight;
And, like the life we honor here,
Reflect the everlasting light.
1880.

MARGARET FULLER

WRITTEN FOR HER CENTENARY

FATE dropt our Margaret
Into the bitter sea,
A pearl in golden splendor set
For spirit majesty.

Love wore her on his hand
And Friendship in her heart,
She glistened in the jeweled band
Of poesy and Art.

Oh! oft the diver brings
His treasure from the deep,
And out of deadly danger wrings
The gems that monarchs keep.

But never gift so fair
His venturous task repaid,
Not emblems rich that Champions wear
At Holytide displayed.

Th' Egyptian's gem of light
Flashed in the gleaming wine,
A regal jewel stol'n from sight
To grace a pomp divine.

So He who laid our Pearl
Deep in the sapphire sea
Keeps her rare essence in the cup
Of immortality.
1909.

ARCHBISHOP WILLIAMS'S JUBILEE

FIFTY years of faithful service,
Saintly record and renown;
Better than the poet's laurels,
He shall wear the patriarch's crown.

Let the generations gather,
Young and old their tributes blend,
For the orphan calls him father,
And the suffering call him friend.

In the name of God most holy
Did this champion take the field;
For the love of Christ the lowly
Has he ministered and healed.

Benedictions at the altar
Hath he called on many a head;
It is now your turn to bless him
Who has given you heavenly bread.

Let the generations gather!
Thanks and prayers to Heaven ascend,
To the everlasting Father,
For the Master, Teacher, Friend!
1895.

JAMES A. GARFIELD

OUR sorrow sends its shadow round the earth.
So brave, so true! A hero from his birth!
The plumes of Empire moult, in mourning draped,
The lightning's message by our tears is shaped.

Life's vanities that blossom for an hour
Heap on his funeral car their fleeting flower.
Commerce forsakes her temples, blind and dim,
And pours her tardy gold to homage him.

The notes of grief to age familiar grow
Before the sad privations all must know;
But the majestic cadence which we hear
To-day, is new in either hemisphere.

What crown is this, high hung and hard to reach,
Whose glory so outshines our laboring speech ?
The crown of Honor, pure and unbetrayed;
He wins the spurs who bears the knightly aid.
1881.

JOHN G. WHITTIER

THE chrism of Christ was on his brow,
The sword of Paul within his hand,
As pledged by a Crusader's vow
He met the evil of the land.

Yet with his armfèd presence went
His poet song, of love inspired,
And his rebukes, of stern intent,
With charity divine were fired.

"What ho! thou Quaker grim, come down!
The mob is clamoring for thy blood!"
I do not fear the Martyr's crown
Since Truth must conquer, by the rood.

"How shouldst thou go, thou man of Peace,
Where Tyranny's red banners wave ? "
Until the bitter feud shall cease,
I take my stand beside the slave.

So Michael, with a brow of Heaven,
Trod the brute Satan underneath;
So to each loyal soul is given
The glory of Faith's civic wreath.

And thou wert crowned, when crownfèd were
Thy heart's high wishes for thy kind,
When spirits breathed a purer air,
And light prevailed o'er passions blind.

Thy linked lustres sped away,
Bringing the heavenly hope more near,
While God's great order of our day
Grew to thy earnest sight more clear.

Numbers were gathered in thy train,
The captive helped in sorest need;
And souls that knew a subtler chain,
From iron superstition freed.

The song of labor thou mad'st sweet,
Setting thy tent on ocean beach;
When snow-bound were thy sober feet,
Thy mind essayed her eagle reach.

How shall we yield thee ? Time doth rob
The very oracles divine.'
The heart of love forgets to throb,
Silent and empty is the shrine.

Yet was it burial when men laid
In earth thy reverend fold of dust?
Was thy life ended when they prayed
Above thy grave in trembling trust ?

Nay, with the spirit of thine age
Mingles the breath that did suspire;
And spread on many a radiant page
Abides the wealth of thy desire.

And Freedom seated on her rock
Above the wrecks of Fate o'erthrown,
Thy record holds beyond the shock

Of change, her treasure, and our own.
1892.

WHITTIER

READ AT THE CENTENNIAL CELEBRATION AT HAVERHILL, DE-
CEMBER 17, 1907

A SPIRIT in our midst abode,
A champion, risking life and limb,
With firm intent to bear the load
That Fate had meted out to him:

The burthen of an evil time
That grieved men's souls with forfeit pledge;
The task, t' assail a nation's crime
With weapon of celestial edge.

For still a son of Peace was he,
Servant and master of the lyre;
All bloodless must his warfare be,
Launched all in love his bolts of fire.

Such victories are given to song
As slaughter never may achieve,
When the rapt soul is wooed from wrong
Some heavenly lesson to receive.

I saw him when the locks that crown
Fair youth were heaped above his brow;

His eyes like lustrous jewels shone,

The trifler's world they did not know.
Feathered as from an angel's wing
The arrows of his quiver flew;
A thrill of sorrow they might bring,
A wound, and yet a balsam too.

Soon War's wild music filled the land,
And fields of fight were won and lost,
When grieving Conscience made her stand
To pay the debt of deadly cost.

And many were the days of dole
Before the bitter strife could cease.
But ever that anointed soul
Dwelt in its citadel of Peace.

Thence, like an anthem rising clear,
Rang out the poet's helpful word;
Melodious messages of cheer
Above the battle din were heard.

And years of labor came and went,
But ere he passed the bound of Fate
His days were crowned with high content;
He saw his land regenerate.

Methought that from the Poet's grave
A whisper thrilled the ear, that said:
"Surrender not his music brave,
For while it lives, he is not dead.

"And when, with other sounds of earth
Shall pass the beauty of his rhyme,

Eternity shall keep the worth
Lost from the treasury of Time."

ABBY WILLIAMS MAY

HER feet were ever ready,
Her hand was ever steady;
The onward sweep
Of purpose deep
Disclosed no flaw nor eddy.

On many an errand went she,
To many a trouble bent she,
Such helpful thought,
Such counsel brought,
The bloom of youth thus spent she.

A maiden of high feature,
Of good and glorious nature,
Dear to His heart
Who did impart
Such grace unto His creature.

So may sweet peace betide her
Whose holy laws did guide her,
And all that's blest
In God's dear rest
Be with her and beside her.
1888.

FOR THE FIFTIETH BIRTHDAY OF JAMES FREEMAN CLARKE

APRIL 4, 1860

A WEIGHT I bear, and a task I share,
Of glad and generous sympathy.
These loving hearts have all their parts,
In the spring-song I must echo thee.

Each eloquent soul would keep control
Of the Poet's slender gift of words,
As an instrument that should give consent
To the waiting music of many birds.

But the wings of love that bear above,
Shall help me to bring my burthen near;
And my stammering tongue, leaving half unsung,
Can tell how we prize thee, Master dear.

For these fifty years we thank with tears
The tender hand that hath counted them;
And we thank again for those that remain
Still veiled in God's unseen diadem.

The roses flung, and the incense swung,
Are for youth's bright matins and manhood's prime;
But the tapers are lit for the patient feet
That follow the pensive vesper chime.

Within thy fold, safe as of old,
Still gather us each bright Sabbath morn;
Call home thy sheep, that wander and weep,

Comfort the weary and briar-worn.

That years a score may sweep us o'er,
Walking yet serene the heavenward way,
A loving band, that the shepherd's hand
Brings near the bounds of the brighter day.

Till transfigured quite, in its holy light,
We hear, still clinging close to thee:
"Father, I come to my heavenly home,
With the children thou hast given me."

FOR THE SEVENTIETH BIRTHDAY OF JAMES FREEMAN CLARKE

WHO knocks? Pass on, I pray:
Thou hast mistook the way.
All that I had I gave in days of yore.
If that thy need be great,
Since Age doth me abate, Ask jocund
Youth to help thee from his store.
Yet stay. For whom the feast?
"For one to whom the least
Of what we owe is such fond gratitude
As from the dumb might wring
Attempted uttering, And from thy lips the breath of song renewed."

Then shall my heart indite
Whate'er my hand can write
From out the wasted treasure of my time.
For, silent here to sit,
And fear my failing wit, My soul should count it very near a crime.

'T was thy persuasive thought
My errant fancy caught
When height of wisdom matched not length of years;
When still, with airy schemes,
And many-featured dreams
I wrought at childish tasks with childish tears.

If ever to the good
Of holy womanhood
Mine own with saintlier spirits did aspire,
Where was the lesson writ,
My slumberous sense to hit,
As by thy hand, in characters of fire ?

For such a glittering net
Doth human souls beset,
That from its bonds they have no power to flee,
Till smites that sword of truth
Which owes no error ruth,
And by pain's costly ransom they are free.

'T were idle in this verse
The reasons to rehearse
For which we crown to-day thy front beloved.
Thou didst thy life impart
With such a gracious art,
We scarcely knew the spell by which we moved.

What nuptials hast thou blest!
What dear ones laid to rest!
What infants welcomed with the holy sign !
Life's hospitality

Was so akin to thee,
That half of all our good and ill was thine.

In dark, perplexing days,
When sorrow silenced praise,
We saw thy light above the vapors dim,
In battle's din and shout
Thy clarion blast rang out:
"The victory is God's, we follow Him."

Thy life has had, like ours,
Its sunshine and its showers,
Has reached the heights of joy, the depths of grief;
But richer hath it been
By all the gifts serene
That make the leader, brother, friend, and chief.

Bring then the palm and vine,
Roses with lilies twine,
And let us image in our offered wreath
The life enriched with toil,
The consecrating oil,
And love that fears not time, and knows not death.

READ AT THE ONE HUNDREDTH ANNIVERSARY OF HIS BIRTH,
CHURCH OP THE DISCIPLES, BOSTON, APRIL 3, 1910

RICHER gift can no man give
Than he doth from God receive.
We in greatness would have pleasure,
But we must accept our measure.
Let us question, then, the grave,
Querying what the Master gave,

Whom, in his immortal state,
Grateful love would celebrate.

Only human life was his,
With its thin-worn mysteries.
Shall we not describe him, "Man,
Built to last a little span, Like our
Earth, his dwelling-place,
Swung aloft, 'twixt Time and Space,
Tuned for ecstasy and pain,
Ever prompted to attain
For the blessing or the curse
That Eternities rehearse ? "
Lifting from the Past its veil,
What of his does now avail?

Just a mirror in his breast
That revealed a heavenly guest,
And the love that made us free
Of the same high company.
These he brought us, these he left
When we were of him bereft.

He was resolute and bright,
Was a hero in the fight,
Trained his gifts of speech and song
Holy lessons to prolong,
Made the great Apostle's dream
Present still and potent seem.
Human fortunes we must share,
Must endeavor, must forbear;
Days of weakness, nights of pain,
Try, and turn, and try again;

But Golconda has no mine
Could that legacy outshine,
Did we keep, through good and ill,
James Freeman's angel with us still.

LUCY STONE

FULL of honors and of years,
Lies our friend at rest,
Passing from earth's hopes and fears
To the ever Blest
One of the anointed few
Touched with special grace
For a life whose service true
Should redeem the race.

Where is that persuasive tone
Welcome in our ears?
Still I hear it, sounding on,
Through the golden spheres.

When we raise our battle cry
For the holy Right,
We shall feel her drawing nigh
With a spirit's might.

As the veil of flesh doth part,
We behold her rise,
Crowned with majesty of heart:
There true queendom lies.
1893.

IN MEMORIAM OTTO DRESEL

HANDEL'S LARGO[3]

ON every shining stair an angel stood,
And to our dear one said, " Walk higher, friend!"
Till, rapt from earth, in a celestial mood,
He passed from sight to blessings without end;
And where his feet had trod, a radiant flood
His lofty message of content did send.

BEETHOVEN'S FUNERAL MARCH[4]

THE heavy steps that 'neath new burdens tread,
The heavy hearts that wait upon the dead,
The struggling thoughts that single out, through
tears, The happy memories of bygone years, And on the deaf and silent presence call:
O friend belov'd! O master! is this all?
But as the cadence moves, the song-flowers fling

To us the promise of eternal spring,
Love that survives the wreck of its delight,
And goes, torch-bearing, into darksome night.
Trumpet and drum have marked the victor's way,
The seraph voices now their legend say:

3   Suggested by Mr. Loeffler's rendering of the " Largo" at a concert especially dedicated to the memory of Otto Dresel, musician and critic, Boston Music Hall, October II,1890.

4   The funeral march from Beethoven's "Eroica" made part of the programme at this concert.

"O loving friends! refrain your waiting fond;
The gates are passed, and heaven is bright beyond."

TO MARY[5]

THOU gracious atom, verging to decay,
What wert thou in the moment of thy stay?
The flowers in thy faded hands that lie
More briefly than thyself scarce bloom and die.
How was it when swift feet thy beauty bore,
And Life's warm ripple sunned thy marble o'er?

A slender maiden, captured by a kiss,
Wed at the altar for a three years' bliss.
No longer space my life's indenture gave
From Juliet's courtship to Ophelia's grave.
The modest helper of heroic art,
The Heaven-bound anchor of a sinking heart.

Ask him who wooed me, earliest and last,
What was my office in Love's sacred past?
What was she, here in silken shell empearled
But my life's life, the comfort of the world?

PHILLIPS BROOKS

THE Christ within the Christ thy heart doth feel,
Without, the Christ-beloved humanity;
And so thy simple, fluent words reveal
What flesh and blood have not made known to thee.

5   Written after attending the funeral of Mary Devlin Booth, wife of Edwin Booth.

As free of evil dost thou wander o'er
This thorny, blooming earth, as if she ne'er
The seeds of sin in her hot bosom bore,
But only treasures consecrate and rare.

Thou treadest fearlessly where Youth and Age
Their pitfalls find, sore wondering at the same;
All doors are open to thy summons sage,
Ice barriers melt before thy touch of flame.

Give us thy secret. Do not flit from earth
Burying the knowledge that hath made thee wise.
Or, if we cannot reach its priceless worth,
Redeem us in the judgment of the skies!

A HEART OFFERING TO THE DEAD BISHOP

PHILLIPS BROOKS

LABOR cease!
Rest and peace
O'er thy silent bed;
Lilies sweet At thy feet,
Lilies at thy head.

Organ boom
In the gloom
Of the darkened shrine;
Hearts whose grief
Seek relief
From the source divine.

Happy years Seen thro' tears,
When he led you all,
In the fields
The gospel yields
With a shepherd's call.

Where he trod,
Love of God
Blossomed into light
Form and hue
Goodlier grew
In the eternal light.

Noblest friend,
Who shall end
All thy tender praise?
Souls alift
With thy shrift
Seeking better ways.

Oh I that rhyme
Could but divine
Something of his worth;
Could upbuild
What God willed
Should be dear on earth I

Keep the word
You have heard
As a fruitful seed;
In the rest
Of Heaven's best,
That shall be his meed.

January 25,1893.

MY FIRST THOUGHT ON HEARING OF BROWNING'S DEATH

CARVE ye two pillows of marble stone
Where Westminster arches stand lofty and lone.
Trace on them two garlands of laurel fair,
And where wedded sovereigns sculptured are,
Make a bed in the holiest aisle,
Where storied windows may glow and smile,
And anthems sing for the Royal Dead,
Sovereigns of song, forever wed.

Fruitful of life were those nuptials rare;
A long train follows the kingly pair,
Over the continents, over the seas,
Far as sunrise can follow the breeze,
Far as sunlight in the sky
Makes human hearts leap glad and high.
Spirits of women, spirits of men,
Spirits in joy and spirits in pain,
Whether for merriment, music, or dole,
Follow the tread of each royal soul.

Open your gates, Westminster high!
Where should the minstrel sovereigns lie?
Walk at their funeral, woman lone,
They have thrilled at your grief and moan.
Wits of all ages, counsellors, kings!
Your thoughts to them were familiar things.
Bane of men's evilness, virtue sublime,

Beauties of childhood, gathered in rhyme,
With this sad pageant their ministry ends.
These were your guardians, these were your friends!
Who shall precede you with dutiful feet ?
Who shall intone for you melodies sweet ?
No one inherits your magical song
That to all ages, all climes doth belong.
Great ones salute you from out the dim past,
Bards of the centuries, fashioned to last.
Homer and Dante and Shakespeare may say:
Souls of 6ur temper are with us to-day.

[N. B. These lines were scrawled, almost illegibly, in the Pullman, on my way, I think, to Fresno, Cal.

Hearing that Browning had died in Venice, the following lines came to me, and were scribbled in like manner, before seeing any account of the procession which they in a manner prefigure.]

Methought I saw our poet's funeral pass
Like a mysterious vision in a glass.
Hearsed in a gondola his ashes lay,
While smiled on him the bright Venetian day,
And silence waited on the bargeman's oar,
Listening for glorious song that comes no more.

The ancient palaces, so primly white,
Did seem to have their sorrow in the sight;
While "in a balcony" lovers and Queen
Persist in acting out their mimic scene,
Scarce heeding when the poet's dust floats by,
Except to say: "Die thou — we need not die.
" The barks fly past, for pleasure, profit, sin,

Urged by some eager hand their goal to win.
For haste thy rowers' muscles are not strained,
No need to hurry now — thou hast attained.
But in thy track a flight of loosened doves,
Other than those thy Venice feeds and loves,
Make plaintive music with their tender call.
Who are ye then, ye creatures slight and small ?
What place in this sad festival have ye?
"We're the song-spirits that his verse did free.
The earth shall hide his dust, for which you grieve,
But in his song a better earth shall live."

MICHAEL ANAGNOS

VAINLY we listen for his tread,
Returning from a distant shore.
Here, where his fruitful days were sped,
The friend beloved is seen no more.

Truly, it was a gracious gift
That Greece vouchsafed us, when he came
With buoyant step and heart alight
To win an enviable fame.

The oracles of Hellas old,
The dream of glories yet to be
Had taught his spirit, frank and bold,
The price and worth of liberty.

He entered where a champion crowned
His noble conquests still pursued,
For him the clarion blast did sound
That stirred the elder Hero's blood.

Where souls in shadows dim abode,
Ungladdened by the light of day,
His tutelary guidance showed
The light of Truth's all conquering ray;

For they should know the world so fair,
Its record brave, its wondrous plan,
And, though despoiled of Nature, share
The great inheritance of man.

Oh! friends who gather in the class
The welcome word to hear and tell,
Take with you, as you onward pass,
The thought of him who loved you well.

That love which doth all ills redeem,
Which seals man's noblest promise true,
The prophet's pledge, the poet's dream,
Be that his legacy to you.
1906.

MARY A. LIVERMORE

THE darkening of a brow belov'd,
The silence of a voice of cheer
That roused, reminded and reproved
For many a day, in many a year.

She stood beside the beds of pain
Where fainting soldiers scarce drew breath;
She won them back to life again,
Or smiled away the pangs of death.

When Duty bade the woman speak,
How bravely did she heed the call!
With presence resolute, yet meek,
She graced the temple and the hall.

Three decades of laborious years,
Their holiday, the light of home;
Their record in the past appears,
Their promise, in the days to come.

For every earnest word she spake
Shall in Time's furrows ripen seed;
The labor shall our world awake
To take deep thought for human need.

We meet in sorrow at her grave,
Right lovingly we say farewell;
All richer for the life she gave,
All poorer for its broken spell.
1905.

WORDSWORTH

BARE of the unseen haven,
Mind of unearthly mood,
Like to the prophet's raven,
Thou bringest me heavenly food;
Or like some mild dove winging
Its way from cloudless skies,
Celestial odors bringing, And in its glad soul singing
The songs of paradise.

Surely thou hast been nearer
The bounds of day and night —
Thy vision has been clearer,
And loftier thy flight,
And thou to God art dearer
Than many men of might.
Speak! for to thee we listen
As never to bard before,
And faded eyes shall glisten
That thought to be bright no more.

Oh, tell us of yonder heaven,
And the world that lies within;
Tell of the happy spirits
To whom we are near of kin;
Tell of the songs of rapture,
Of the stars that never set;
Do the angels call us brothers —
Does our Father love us yet?

Speak, for our souls are thirsting
For the light of righteousness;
Speak, for our bosoms are bursting
With a desolate loneliness;
Our hearts are worn and weary,
Our robes are travel-soiled —
For through a desert dreary
Our wandering feet have toiled.

Those to whom life looks brighter
May ask an earthlier strain:
A gayer spell and a lighter
Shall hold them in its chain;

But to those who have drunk deepest
Of the cup of joy and grief,
The tuneful tears thou weepest
Do minister relief.

Speak, for the earth is throbbing
With a wild sense of pain;
The wintry winds are sobbing
The requiem of the slain;
Dimly our lamps are burning,
And gladly we list to thee,
With a strange and mystic yearning
Toward the home where we would be:
Turn from the rhyme of weary Time,
And sing of Eternity!

Tell of the sacred mountains
Where prophets in prayer have kneeled;
Tell of the glorious fountains
That soon shall be unsealed;
Tell of the quiet regions
Where those we love are fled;
Tell of the angel legions
That guard the blessèd dead!

Tell of the sea of glass,
And of the icy river;
To those who its waves must pass
Thy message of love deliver.
Strike, strike thy harp of many lays,
And we will join the song of praise
To Him that sitteth upon the throne
Of life and love forever.

Written many yean ago.

LEONARD MONTEFIORE

BY a way of pain and fire
Laid across thy heart's desire,
Thou hast swift arrival where
Ends for thee all earthly care.
From the dismal darkened room,
Where thou cam'st in manhood's bloom,
Where thy vigils of distress
Faded into nothingness,
Men a lifeless burthen carry
For a voyage that may not tarry.

Thou in noble house wert bred,
Wisdom stood thy youth in stead,
Features of an ancient race
Looked in beauty from thy face.
T was thy early wont to sit
With the men of lofty wit,
Hear the counsels that outshine
Ruby gem and ruby wine.

Wail of kindred o'er the sea
Wakes our sorrowing sympathy,
And the hospitable land
That would take thee by the hand
Sadly yields thee to the wave
That doth bar thy island grave.

In this loss, so sad and cold,

Comfort we would still behold,
And, in this divorce of death,
Look beyond the failing breath.
For the doors of human pride
And illusion, opening wide,
Loose thee from this fabled scene,
To the steadfast life serene.
Prophet of the ancient psalm
Usher thee to holy calm.
On the heights where Moses trod
May thy soul commune with God.

Snows of age shall never rest
Heavy on thy manly crest.
Thro' no waning nor decay
Doth thy swift soul wing its way.
All the promise that we knew
Shall remain forever true.
And the gift that we surrender
With a spasm dear and tender
Goes to hands that never waste
What we give with grief and haste,
Till the Giver gives again
Life for death, and joy for pain.

FOUND IN ENVELOPE MASKED

THE LOST POEM

1907

MASTER that dwell'st in peace serene,
Thrice happy soul, that ours hast been,

We turn to thee in this fair scene;

As birds that pipe around a cage
Seek its loved inmate to engage
In the sweet war that singers wage.

But thou from out the golden wires
Hast passed, beyond the sunset fires,
To enter where our thought aspires.

Well we recall the falling snows,
The sad day darkening to its close
That saw thee folded in repose.

And as they led thy funeral train
Fair rhymes, the children of thy brain,
Did follow thee with hushed refrain.

In marble shall men set thy name,
Give lavish measure to thy claim
For dear remembrance and high fame.

FREDERIC LAWRENCE KNOWLES

A GENTLE presence is removed,
The face and form of one beloved.
He in our revels bore his part,
He was a brother of the heart.

Before his gracious youth could pass
Its vision vanished from the glass.
The hand that for high merit strove
Returns no more the clasp of love.

But ere he passed, the sacred bays
Lent their deep meaning to his ways;
His glowing strophes did resound,
He lived and died, a poet crowned,
Happy to lisp with parting breath
A music that may challenge Death.

POEMS OF SENTIMENT AND REFLECTION

FROM MY NURSERY

FORTY-SIX YEARS AGO

WHEN I was a little child,
Said my passionate nurse, and wild:
"Wash you, children, clean and white;
God may call you any night."

Close my tender brother clung,
While I said with doubtful tongue:
"No, we cannot die so soon;
For you told, the other noon,

Of those months in order fine
That should make the earth divine.
I've not seen, scarce five years old,
Months like those of which you told."

Softly, then, the woman's hand
Loosed my frock from silken band,
Tender smoothed the fiery head,
Often shamed for ringlets red.

Somewhat gently did she say,
"Child, those months are every day."

Still, methinks, I wait in fear,
For that wonder-glorious year —
For a spring without a storm,
Summer honey-dewed and warm,
Autumn of robuster strength,
Winter piled in crystal length.

I will wash me clean and white;
God may call me any night.
I must tell him when I go
His great year is yet to know —
Year when workings of the race
Shall match Creation's dial face;
Each hour be born of music's chime,
And Truth eternal told in Time.

ROUGE GAGNE

THE wheel is turned, the cards are laid;
The circle's drawn, the bets are made:
I stake my gold upon the red.

The rubies of the bosom mine,
The river of life, so swift divine,
In red all radiantly shine.

Upon the cards, like gouts of blood,
Lie dinted hearts, and diamonds good,
The red for faith and hardihood.

In red the sacred blushes start
On errand from a virgin heart,
o win its glorious counterpart.

The rose that makes the summer fair,
The velvet robe that sovereigns wear,
The red revealment could not spare.

And men who conquer deadly odds
By fields of ice, and raging floods,
Take the red passion from the gods.

Now Love is red, and Wisdom pale,
But human hearts are faint and frail
Till Love meets Love, and bids it hail.

I see the chasm, yawning dread:
I see the flaming arch o'erhead:
I stake my life upon the red.

THE OPEN DOOR
THE Master said, " I am the Door.
The world is dark with doubt and sin,
Hidden the good that men implore,
But after me ye enter in.

" The ancient barriers I disown,
The distant and the dark control,
Who with your onward steps have thrown
God's sunshine open to the soul."

Another mystic door I know,
The entrance to this world of ours,

And she who opens it bears low
A wondrous weight of pains and powers.

O men that plan the stately pile,
Where law and learning hold their sway,
And drive with subterfuge and wile
Your mothers from the door away, —

Undo the doors! In God's high noon
An equal heritage have we;
Your cold exclusion's out of tune With Nature's hospitality.

See where the word of freedom lives
To bridge the gulf of ages o'er;
Learn how the Eternal Giver gives,
And keep with Christ the open door !

RAFAEL'S ST. CECILIA

METHINKS a wondrous harmony
Doth through the ether fall;
My heart, attuned to heavenly joy,
Makes answer to its call.

A breath divine is in this sky,
So limpid and so blue;
A radiance, streaming from on high,
Makes all things fair and new.

The mighty rhythm of the spheres
But echoes His behest
Who bids Devotion build her shrine
Deep in the faithful breast.

The music welcomes low and sweet
The Presence drawing nigh;
Sing, brothers, sing; with measure meet
Salute Heaven's majesty!

A SCRAP[6]
METHHTCS my friends grow beauteous in my sight,
As the years make their havoc of sweet things;
Like the intenser glory of the light
When the sad bird of Autumn sits and sings.

Ah! woe is me! ah! Memory, Be cheerful, thanking God for things that be.

A DREAM OF THE HEARTHSTONE

A FIGURE by my fireside stayed,
Plain was her garb, and veiled her face;
A presence mystical she made,
Nor changed her attitude, nor place.

Did I neglect my household ways
For pleasure, wrought of pen or book?
She sighed a murmur of dispraise,
At which, methought, the rafters shook.

Me young Delight did often win
My patient limits to outgo.
Thereafter, when I entered in
That shrouded guest did warning show.

---

6   I think this dates as far back as X857. I copy it in 1882;

The snows of Age to chill me fell
(Where many a gracious mate lay dead),
And moved my heart to break the spell
By that ungracious phantom laid.

"Now, who art thou that didst not smile
When I my maddest jest devised ?
Who art thou, stark and grim the while
That men my time and measure prized ?"

Without her pilgrim staff she rose,
Her weeds of darkness cast aside;
More dazzling than Olympian snows
The beauty that those weeds did hide.

Most like a solemn symphony
That lifts the heart from lowly things,
The voice with which she spake to me
Did loose contrition at its springs.

"Oh Duty! Visitor divine,
Take all the wealth my house affords,
But make thy holy methods mine;
Speak to me thy surpassing words!

" Neglected once and undiscerned,
I pour my homage at thy feet.
Till I thy sacred law have learned
Nor joy, nor life can be complete."

FLOWERS

THE flowers are sure his teachers

Who learns their varied speech,
And wondrous are the sermons
The friendly blossoms preach.

The Winter bids them vanish;
They close their friendly eyes,
And wait the joyous sentence
When Spring shall bid them rise.

They say, "Look up to heaven
With ever-radiant face,
Transmute earth's waste and rubbish
To purity and grace.

" Our roots may know dark secrets,
But these we do not tell;
When peevish zephyr questions,
We answer, 'All is well.'

" Whether we deck the wedding
Or garland o'er the bier,
Comes still the steadfast message:
The end of all's not here.

" Pursue the humble wisdom
Wherewith God makes us wise,
And answer back his sentence
With hope that never dies."

A SNAP SHOT

WHO is this sprite so dainty,
At odds with grisly Death ?

His struggles nought avail him,
The Conqueror conquereth.

"Oh! I am one whose heeding
Was all of delights most high;
Time's treasures fitly feeding
My delicate sense and eye."

But say, didst thou feed others?
"My lovers, and my friends."
And never a dusty beggar? i
Then here thy banquet ends!

A LEGEND OF BRITTANY

IN Carnac's field a silent army stands,
Stands without feet and signals without hands;
No human feature crowns their upright form;
Nor human impulse their stern height doth warm.

Cornely, holy man, remembered here,
To every hornèd beast a guardian dear,
Was one day followed by a heathen band,
Who to ensnare his sacred life had planned.

Seaward he fled, but when the strand he neared,
Nor helpful skiff, nor friendly sail appeared.
Then in his hearing some one seemed to say:
"Thou man of God, wherefore dost flee away?
Stand fast and show on this appointed spot,
The puissance which thy heathen foe have not."

Then turned Comely, then erect he stood,

And held on high the symbol of the Rood,
While from the skies a voice said audibly:
"Your hearts are stone, stone let your bodies be."

So, carved in granite, did their features fade,
Of each stark form a monument was made;
There, in stern drill, they wait the Judgment day,
When the Saint's prayers may melt their bonds away,

THE ECHO

DREAMED IN A SOLITARY EVENING, MARCH 4, 1905.

GOD gave the echo, that no beauteous sound
Should e'er without its counterpart be found.
So, where angelic melody has birth,
It wakes its partner ere it flits from earth.

A monarch wears upon his diadem
The rainbow, prisoned in an opal gem.
Ev'n so, all glories of sea and sky
Captive in Man's imagination lie.

With them the boundless aeons of the past,
And future dim that should forever last.
So, one may think our Lord his crown doth make
Of such soul gems, and wears them for our sake.

AMONG MY TREES

HAIL, thou hundred-handed pine,
Swaying with a grace divine,

Light and heat and air receiving,
Beauty and soft fragrance giving.

Teach us music, songful birds,
With your seconds and your thirds;
Melodies intangible,
From past times infrangible;
You could tell us if you dared,
If you only knew we cared;

Handing down the mystery
Of timeless human history
That unwritten never was,
Never told its end or cause.

ALL SAINTS

MY mind reviews the story
Of the old primeval glory:
Of Abram, whom on Midian's plain
God heard, and answered to again;
Of Moses from the sweep of Nile
Saved by a sister's tender wile;

The captains and the seers of old, Whom
God's anointing made so bold;
The pure faith-jewel handed down
Till cross and scourging brought its crown.

Kindred to these, tho' in time apart,
The loves ancestral of my heart,
The ancient grandsire, parents sage,
My fair son, nip't in tender age,

And one, now lying still and lone,
A daughter, to a sister grown.
Such memories gild, with glowing ray,
The passage of this All Saints' Day.
1885.

A WAGE-EARNER

THEY were twining wreaths of laurel
For many an honored head,
And spreading cloth of crimson
For princely feet to tread,
And singing in loud triumph
The paean of the hour,
The joy of recent conquest,
The victor's praise and power;

When one came by heart-weary
With service of the day:
"From dawn to dusk I've labored,
Where do such have their pay ?"

Back of this gay assemblage,
Unnoticed of the crowd,
Leadeth a narrow passage
Which darkling shadows shroud.

It smells not of the laurel
Nor shows the carpet fine;
There shalt thou find the Master,
And there receive his coin.

A penny of old fashion

With marks of sweat and blood;
Such Moses took in payment,
And Christ, who blessed the rood.

Clean hands of many a martyr
Have held this symbol small,
Bequeathing to the ages
The value of their all.

And fairer in the using
Of centuries it grows;
Among immortal treasures,
Splendid and sole it shows.

Be joyful in receiving
From heavenly Lord and Friend '
What falsehood cannot gather
And folly cannot spend.

Mined from the heart of ages,
Stamped with unerring skill,
It heaven and earth can purchase,
God's service, man's good-will.

WICKED PATIENCE

SWEET Christ, with flagellations brought
To thine immortal martyrdom,
Cancel the bitter treasons wrought
By men who bid thy kingdom come.

Their sinful blood we may not urge,
While Mercy stays thy righteous hand;

But take all ours, if that should purge
The wicked patience of the land!

THE WORLD MESSENGER

MARCH 26, 1905

WHO comes with tidings from afar?
What says the peasant, what the Czar?
In farthest East, where fearful strife
Pours Nation's blood for Nation's life?
How fare the armies madly matched?
What new conspiracies are hatched
In that dark house where counsels lag
While fierce Rebellion waves her flag?

Still does complacent Europe smirk
At the pledged promise of the Turk?
As fruitless as their sympathies
Who rail at his iniquities,
But never yet have plucked up heart
To act a valiant Champion's part !

On our own shores, what new surprise?
What forecast, both of fools and wise?
What covert heaping of the spoil ?
What protest of hard-handed toil?
What Sunday sentences of good?
What Monday floating with the flood?

Questions like these, and many more Are answered at our very door.
Who is it that thus daily reads

The riddle of our human needs?
What giant with a million hands,
With feet familiar in all lands,
Tracks through this world the flight of Fame,
Rehearsed to us for praise or blame?
Who is this Master-Servant? Guess.
What is it but The Daily Press!

A NEW FLAG[7]

WE'LL have a new flag, my brothers — we'll have a new flag, my boys !
Since swords have been ground to ploughshares, and trumpets are turned to toys;
We have had enough of the red stripe, the planet of war is set,
And in the blue empyrean, the white steeds of peace are met.

Their reins are of starry silver, their hoofs are of virgin gold,
They carry our fates behind them, in a master's steady hold;
The armies of retribution strode heavily to the sea,
But the message of consolation shall winged and
wafted be.

We'll have the Christ on our banner, the hero of truth and toil;
Not a miser meting his treasure, not a victor counting his spoil;
The Christ that to lords and peasants sent equal command and call,

Who throned in the skiff or palace, Hope's master and Sorrow's thrall.
We'll measure the fields together where Labor was maimed and dumb;
Where shadows wrought in the furrows, whose sunshine at last has come.
Where the sense of the nation slumbered, in spiritless sloth and shame,'
Till with flashing of arms and torches, the terrible bridegroom came.

---

7   Written soon after the close of the Civil War.

The forum shall stand for justice, and the temples shall stand for prayer
Whose answer the arm may hasten, not cast on the viewless air;
Not crowded to distant heaven the humble and poor shall wait;
For heaven shall be seen among us, the happy, immortal state.

And we 'll build the gladsome schoolhouse, where small angels unawares
Are trained at the desk of duty, or seated on studious chairs,
And sowing that seed most sacred, in the young and teeming ground,
We shall look for a precious harvest, a nation redeemed and sound;

We'll straiten the yoke of duty, and doctrine make one for all;
Each may hope for and do his utmost, by his own worth stand or fall;
We'll not lift men for their features, nor lower them for their skin;
But look to the great soul-Father, in whom we are all of kin.

And why do we strive for riches, since all are in Thine possessed ?
And why are we mad for honors, when true service honors best ?
And why should we build up limits, dividing the land's fair face ?
They are one — her brow and her bosom!
They are one, her growth and her grace.

So we'll have a new flag, my brothers! our stripes, we have felt them all;
Our stars in the dusk of battle did mournfully pale and fall;
Let us yield our claims and our quarrels for a compact of priceless worth;
For the peace that Christ found in heaven, the peace that he left on earth.

SONG OF THE HAREBELL

AS I FOUND IT ON AN ALPINE SLOPE

SPRING is coming,
Birds are humming,
Streamlets skipping,

Maidens tripping.

Touch me slightly,
Wave me lightly,
Ding a ding,
This is spring.

This new-comer
Men call summer,
With a color
Flashing fuller,
With a splendor
Fresh and tender.

Touch me warmly,
Uniformly,
Summer sings
Of steadfast things.

Autumn's here now,
Leaves are sere now,
Ice-chains forging,
No more gorging
Of the bee's throat,
Of the wild goat.

Ring a knell
I Summer fell

See the summit!
Winter from it
Sends its hoary
Glittering glory.

Snow doth bind me,
You'll not find me.
Silence praises;
God amazes.

NIGHT THOUGHTS

I

'T is our sun's light that returns
Where flame-cinctured Saturn burns.

'T is our Holy One whose grace
Shines in each illumined face.

Lavish Noon lies all abroad,
Midnight doth her treasures hoard.

Thro' close darkness oft is won
Highest light of soul or sun.

II

Night her starry gems doth hoar,
Day's delights are freely poured,
Yet is beautiful the play
Of succeeding Night and Day,
Sun and shadow, work and rest,
And the star-lamps for God's guest

TO AN INFANT OF DAYS

No foot hast thou for frolic or for speed,
No brain to plan for conquest or for need;
No hand to work Man's miracles of skill,
Nor wise discernment, parting good from ill.
Yet none can say how high thy strength shall lift,
How wondrous and beneficent thy gift.
O grant, mysterious Powers, that this may prove
A riddle of fair omen, writ in love!

HUMANITY[8]

METHOUGHT a moment that I stood
Where hung the Christ upon the Cross,
Just when mankind had writ in blood
The record of its dearest loss.

The bitter drink men offered him
His kingly gesture did decline,
And my heart sought, in musing dim,
Some cordial for those lips divine. "

When lo! a cup of purest gold
My trembling fingers did uphold;
Within it glowed a wine as red
As hearts, not grapes, its drops had shed.
Drink deep, my Christ, I offer thee
The ransom of Humanity.

BUILDING

I SAT before Fate's ebbing tide

8   Marked, " Writ some time this summer, 1905, at Oak Glen."

With my life's buildings near at hand,
And thought, how planned in marble pride
Was that which crumbled in the sand.
While the soul's Master-architect
Held me to reason and reflect.

"Oh! Master, I have wrought so ill
Would heaven I had not wrought at all!
So petty my devising skill,
My measures so unjust and small."

"But didst thou build for God ? " said He.
"Then doth God's building stand for thee."

QUATRAINS

I

WOULDST thou on me but turn thy wondrous sight,
My breast would be so flooded by thy light,
The light whose language is immortal song,
That I to all the ages should belong.[9]

II

I gave my son a palace,
And a kingdom to control;
The palace of his body,
The kingdom of his soul.

[9] July 25,1908. The thought came to me that if God only looked upon me, I should become radiant, like a star.

IN MUSIC HALL[9]

LOOKING DOWN UPON THE WHITE HEADS OF MY CONTEMPORARIES

BENEATH what mound of snow
Are hid my springtime roses ?
How shall Remembrance know
Where buried Hope reposes ?

In what forgetful heart
As in a canon darkling,
Slumbers the blissful art
That set my heaven sparkling ?

What sense shall never know,
Soul shall remember;
Roses beneath the snow,
June in November.

ON THE DEATH OF A FRIEND
THINK of one who comes no more
To our circle glad and gay.
Once, she gave us of her store,
Shared our simple holiday.

Silent, to the silent land
Was her gentle spirit's flight,'
From our earth ball, bound and shunned,
To the realm of endless light.

---

9   Written years ago. Found Nov. 29th, 1901, and here copied.

To the aeons that replace
Well our paltry tale of years,
To the truth's unclouded face,
To the music of the spheres.

Well equipt our friend might seem
For that sudden, mystic change.
To her patient soul, we deem
Heavenly greetings were not strange.

Freed from days of suff'ring drear,
From the torment of her pain,
She is still a presence here,
In our love she lives again.

THE CHRIST

COMMUNION, CHANNING MEMORIAL CHURCH

I HAVE grasped to-day a hand outstretched
Long since, for human weal;
Its gesture strong for righteousness,
Its mercy swift to heal.

Unto the question of my soul
Its touch an answer gives;
I asked of God: "Is Christ with Thee ?"
It answers: "Still he lives.

"The glory of the world you love
Comes of the life he led;
You feel its radiance everywhere,
And ask if he is dead ?"

Then to my thought that hand of help
A golden net did spread
Wherein were all we deem alive,
And all whom we call dead.

And, as I looked, a voice did say:
"Harm not a single mesh;
It holds in harmony divine
All spirit and all flesh."

THE PEACE CONGRESS

THE legendary ark of yore
Sent forth a pilgrim dove
Whose pinions fair a message bore,
An embassy of love.

Where first her foot did rest, was found
The olive branch of Peace,
And, waving this o'er Ocean's bound,
She bade its tumult cease.

Again, when Jesus, strong to save,
By Jordan's tide did wait,
A white dove hovered o'er the wave
His form should consecrate.;

The blazonry of discord glows
In the ensanguined East,
And man with man must meet as foes,
As beast encounters beast.

But human souls have power to seek
The majesty of prayer,
And, quickened by its might, to speak
Words that sound everywhere.

From these calm precincts where we meet
Intent on heavenly things,
The Dove of Peace the world shall greet
With healing on her wings. 1904.

IN THE STREET

Along the way bright chariots rolled,
With pleasure-seekers, gay and bold.
The throng passed by and knew me not,
The service of my life forgot.

The flush of youth, the pride of wealth,
Broadly displayed, though gained by stealth,
All, all their eager game pursued.
Neglected in the street I stood.

In a poor attic, overhead,
Were certain maids who sewed for bread,
Cheering their work with songs of mine.
Musing, I cried, "Rich gifts may please,
But where are givers like to these
Who, without knowledge or design,
Here crown me with a joy divine?"

NOVEMBER

ALL in a chamber
Besprent with amber
The parting Year his guests receives.
His sunsets tender
Their robes of splendor;
Still is he crowned with golden leaves.

While yet he lingers
The Frost's swift fingers
Are weaving him his wintry shroud;
A pall descending
With crystal blending
Shall veil his forests, slumber-bowed.

Beyond this curtain
His end is certain.
Why, then, does he still smile and sing ?
Because a vision
Of hope elysian Reveals the promise of the spring.
1909.

SIX PRETTY CRADLES

I HAVE tended six pretty cradles,
With the prettiest babes within;
All heart-flames of holy rapture
In a world of grief and sin.

Six cradles make six coffins;

I see them as I sit. In giving life
I have given death —
Thus sorrow and solace knit!

Six babes may make six angels;
Oh! grant it, God of grace,
That, lifted on their loving wings,
I too may see Thy face!
1909.

CHRISTMAS

IN highest heaven a new-born star
Unveils its radiance from afar;
The while, upon her first-born child,
The mother of an hour has smiled.

To what a rustic nursery
Cometh this dear nativity!
No hostelry our Babe receives.
Upon the refuse of the sheaves
Is pillowed that sweet forehead, born
To feel the sharpness of the thorn.

Pious souls, in Orient warned,
Seek the Presence unadorned.
Journeying far, they would inquire
Where doth rest the mystic fire
That shall ravish land and sea
With a new divinity.

Regal gifts the pilgrims bear, —
Gold and myrrh and incense rare.

Soon the offered sweet perfume
Consecrates the stable room:
While, from out the wintry gloom,
Leaping Dawn uplights the skies,
Shows the Babe to reverent eyes.

Soon thou, dear Child, wilt leave thy play,
Mimic dance, and roundelay;
By some deep whisper in thy breast
Sent on Truth's immortal quest;
In thy young reason, tender still,
Shaping the fated fight with ill.

Thou shalt learn the humble trade
That for thee no cradle made;
Eat the peasant's homely fare,
His unfashioned garments wear.
While thy royalty of soul
Doth foreshadow its control
Over ages yet unborn
That shall bless thy natal morn.

Ah, sorrow! that thy fair spring-tide
The martyr's mission must abide,
Thy thought with saintly daring probe
The festering ulcers of the globe;
While reckless multitudes will stand
To pierce and bind thy healing hand,
And thy manhood's fixed intent
Leads to Calvary's ascent.

O joy! that far beyond the cross,
Its bitter pain, its shame and loss,

Above the failure men might see
Truth's endless triumph crowneth thee!
Such a promise in thy birth,
Such a glory come to earth,
Such a tragedy divine
To be wrought in pangs of time,
Such redemption without end, Brother,
Master, Saviour, Friend!

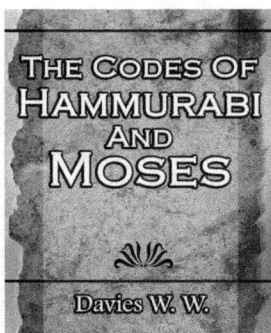

The Codes Of Hammurabi And Moses
W. W. Davies

QTY

The discovery of the Hammurabi Code is one of the greatest achievements of archaeology, and is of paramount interest, not only to the student of the Bible, but also to all those interested in ancient history...

Religion ISBN: *1-59462-338-4* **Pages:132**
MSRP $12.95

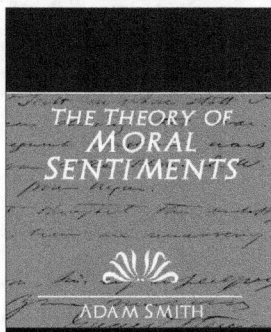

The Theory of Moral Sentiments
Adam Smith

QTY

This work from 1749. contains original theories of conscience amd moral judgment and it is the foundation for systemof morals.

Philosophy ISBN: *1-59462-777-0* **Pages:536**
MSRP $19.95

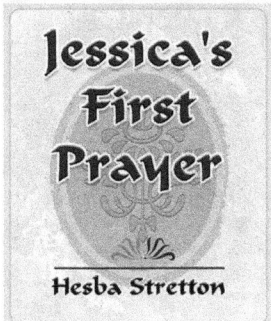

Jessica's First Prayer
Hesba Stretton

QTY

In a screened and secluded corner of one of the many railway-bridges which span the streets of London there could be seen a few years ago, from five o'clock every morning until half past eight, a tidily set-out coffee-stall, consisting of a trestle and board, upon which stood two large tin cans, with a small fire of charcoal burning under each so as to keep the coffee boiling during the early hours of the morning when the work-people were thronging into the city on their way to their daily toil...

Pages:84

Childrens ISBN: *1-59462-373-2* *MSRP $9.95*

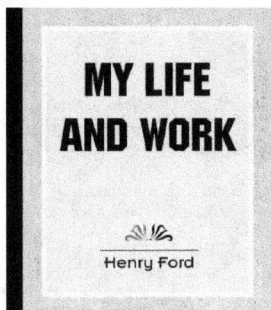

My Life and Work
Henry Ford

QTY

Henry Ford revolutionized the world with his implementation of mass production for the Model T automobile. Gain valuable business insight into his life and work with his own auto-biography... "We have only started on our development of our country we have not as yet, with all our talk of wonderful progress, done more than scratch the surface. The progress has been wonderful enough but..."

Pages:300

Biographies/ ISBN: *1-59462-198-5* *MSRP $21.95*

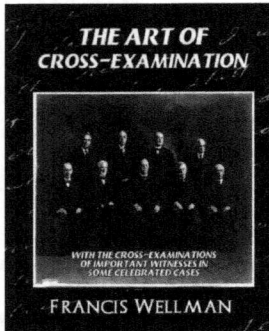

The Art of Cross-Examination
Francis Wellman

QTY

I presume it is the experience of every author, after his first book is published upon an important subject, to be almost overwhelmed with a wealth of ideas and illustrations which could readily have been included in his book, and which to his own mind, at least, seem to make a second edition inevitable. Such certainly was the case with me; and when the first edition had reached its sixth impression in five months, I rejoiced to learn that it seemed to my publishers that the book had met with a sufficiently favorable reception to justify a second and considerably enlarged edition. ..

Pages:412

Reference   **ISBN: *1-59462-647-2***   *MSRP $19.95*

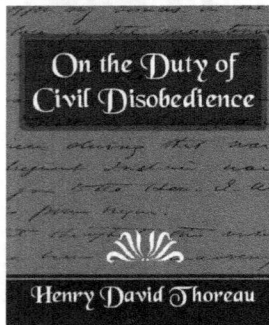

On the Duty of Civil Disobedience
Henry David Thoreau

QTY

Thoreau wrote his famous essay, On the Duty of Civil Disobedience, as a protest against an unjust but popular war and the immoral but popular institution of slave-owning. He did more than write—he declined to pay his taxes, and was hauled off to gaol in consequence. Who can say how much this refusal of his hastened the end of the war and of slavery ?

Law   **ISBN: *1-59462-747-9***   **Pages:48**

MSRP $7.45

Dream Psychology Psychoanalysis for Beginners
Sigmund Freud

QTY

Sigmund Freud, born Sigismund Schlomo Freud (May 6, 1856 - September 23, 1939), was a Jewish-Austrian neurologist and psychiatrist who co-founded the psychoanalytic school of psychology. Freud is best known for his theories of the unconscious mind, especially involving the mechanism of repression; his redefinition of sexual desire as mobile and directed towards a wide variety of objects; and his therapeutic techniques, especially his understanding of transference in the therapeutic relationship and the presumed value of dreams as sources of insight into unconscious desires.

Pages:196

Psychology   **ISBN: *1-59462-905-6***   *MSRP $15.45*

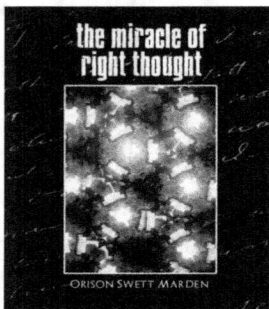

The Miracle of Right Thought
Orison Swett Marden

QTY

Believe with all of your heart that you will do what you were made to do. When the mind has once formed the habit of holding cheerful, happy, prosperous pictures, it will not be easy to form the opposite habit. It does not matter how improbable or how far away this realization may see, or how dark the prospects may be, if we visualize them as best we can, as vividly as possible, hold tenaciously to them and vigorously struggle to attain them, they will gradually become actualized, realized in the life. But a desire, a longing without endeavor, a yearning abandoned or held indifferently will vanish without realization.

Pages:360

Self Help   **ISBN: *1-59462-644-8***   *MSRP $25.45*

QTY

The Rosicrucian Cosmo-Conception Mystic Christianity *by Max Heindel*   ISBN: *1-59462-188-8*   **$38.95**
The Rosicrucian Cosmo-conception is not dogmatic, neither does it appeal to any other authority than the reason of the student. It is: not controversial, but is: sent forth in the, hope that it may help to clear...   New Age/Religion Pages 646

Abandonment To Divine Providence *by Jean-Pierre de Caussade*   ISBN: *1-59462-228-0*   **$25.95**
"The Rev. Jean Pierre de Caussade was one of the most remarkable spiritual writers of the Society of Jesus in France in the 18th Century. His death took place at Toulouse in 1751. His works have gone through many editions and have been republished...   Inspirational/Religion Pages 400

Mental Chemistry *by Charles Haanel*   ISBN: *1-59462-192-6*   **$23.95**
Mental Chemistry allows the change of material conditions by combining and appropriately utilizing the power of the mind. Much like applied chemistry creates something new and unique out of careful combinations the mastery of mental chemistry...   New Age/Business Pages 354

The Letters of Robert Browning and Elizabeth Barret Barrett 1845-1846 vol II   ISBN: *1-59462-193-4*   **$35.95**
by Robert Browning and Elizabeth Barrett   Biographies Pages 596

Gleanings In Genesis (volume I) *by Arthur W. Pink*   ISBN: *1-59462-130-6*   **$27.45**
Appropriately has Genesis been termed "the seed plot of the Bible" for in it we have, in germ form, almost all of the great doctrines which are afterwards fully developed in the books of Scripture which follow...   Religion/Inspirational Pages 420

The Master Key *by L. W. de Laurence*   ISBN: *1-59462-001-6*   **$30.95**
In no branch of human knowledge has there been a more lively increase of the spirit of research during the past few years than in the study of Psychology, Concentration and Mental Discipline. The requests for authentic lessons in Thought Control, Mental Discipline and...   New Age/Occult Pages 422

The Lesser Key Of Solomon Goetia *by L. W. de Laurence*   ISBN: *1-59462-092-X*   **$9.95**
This translation of the first book of the "Lernegton" which is now for the first time made accessible to students of Talismanic Magic was done, after careful collation and edition, from numerous Ancient Manuscripts in Hebrew, Latin, and French...   New Age Pages 92

Rubaiyat Of Omar Khayyam *by Edward Fitzgerald*   ISBN:*1-59462-332-5*   **$13.95**
Edward Fitzgerald, whom the world has already learned, in spite of his own efforts to remain within the shadow of anonymity, to look upon as one of the rarest poets of the century, was born at Bredfield, in Suffolk, on the 31st of March, 1809. He was the third son of John Purcell...   Music Pages 172

Ancient Law *by Henry Maine*   ISBN: *1-59462-128-4*   **$29.95**
The chief object of the following pages is to indicate some of the earliest ideas of mankind, as they are reflected in Ancient Law, and to point out the relation of those ideas to modern thought.   Religion/History Pages 452

Far-Away Stories *by William J. Locke*   ISBN: *1-59462-129-2*   **$19.45**
"Good wine needs no bush, but a collection of mixed vintages does. And this book is just such a collection. Some of the stories I do not want to remain buried for ever in the museum files of dead magazine-numbers an author's not unpardonable vanity..."   Fiction Pages 272

Life of David Crockett *by David Crockett*   ISBN: *1-59462-250-7*   **$27.45**
"Colonel David Crockett was one of the most remarkable men of the times in which he lived. Born in humble life, but gifted with a strong will, an indomitable courage, and unremitting perseverance...   Biographies/New Age Pages 424

Lip-Reading *by Edward Nitchie*   ISBN: *1-59462-206-X*   **$25.95**
Edward B. Nitchie, founder of the New York School for the Hard of Hearing, now the Nitchie School of Lip-Reading, Inc, wrote "LIP-READING Principles and Practice". The development and perfecting of this meritorious work on lip-reading was an undertaking...   How-to Pages 400

A Handbook of Suggestive Therapeutics, Applied Hypnotism, Psychic Science   ISBN: *1-59462-214-0*   **$24.95**
by Henry Munro   Health/New Age/Health/Self-help Pages 376

A Doll's House: and Two Other Plays *by Henrik Ibsen*   ISBN: *1-59462-112-8*   **$19.95**
Henrik Ibsen created this classic when in revolutionary 1848 Rome. Introducing some striking concepts in playwriting for the realist genre, this play has been studied the world over.   Fiction/Classics/Plays 308

The Light of Asia *by sir Edwin Arnold*   ISBN: *1-59462-204-3*   **$13.95**
In this poetic masterpiece, Edwin Arnold describes the life and teachings of Buddha. The man who was to become known as Buddha to the world was born as Prince Gautama of India but he rejected the worldly riches and abandoned the reigns of power when...   Religion/History/Biographies Pages 170

The Complete Works of Guy de Maupassant *by Guy de Maupassant*   ISBN: *1-59462-157-8*   **$16.95**
"For days and days, nights and nights, I had dreamed of that first kiss which was to consecrate our engagement, and I knew not on what spot I should put my lips..."   Fiction/Classics Pages 240

The Art of Cross-Examination *by Francis L. Wellman*   ISBN: *1-59462-309-0*   **$26.95**
Written by a renowned trial lawyer, Wellman imparts his experience and uses case studies to explain how to use psychology to extract desired information through questioning.   How-to/Science/Reference Pages 408

Answered or Unanswered? *by Louisa Vaughan*   ISBN: *1-59462-248-5*   **$10.95**
Miracles of Faith in China   Religion Pages 112

The Edinburgh Lectures on Mental Science (1909) *by Thomas*   ISBN: *1-59462-008-3*   **$11.95**
This book contains the substance of a course of lectures recently given by the writer in the Queen Street Hall, Edinburgh. Its purpose is to indicate the Natural Principles governing the relation between Mental Action and Material Conditions...   New Age/Psychology Pages 148

Ayesha *by H. Rider Haggard*   ISBN: *1-59462-301-5*   **$24.95**
Verily and indeed it is the unexpected that happens! Probably if there was one person upon the earth from whom the Editor of this, and of a certain previous history, did not expect to hear again...   Classics Pages 380

Ayala's Angel *by Anthony Trollope*   ISBN: *1-59462-352-X*   **$29.95**
The two girls were both pretty, but Lucy who was twenty-one who supposed to be simple and comparatively unattractive, whereas Ayala was credited, as her Bombwhat romantic name might show, with poetic charm and a taste for romance. Ayala when her father died was nineteen...   Fiction Pages 484

The American Commonwealth *by James Bryce*   ISBN: *1-59462-286-8*   **$34.45**
An interpretation of American democratic political theory. It examines political mechanics and society from the perspective of Scotsman James Bryce   Politics Pages 572

Stories of the Pilgrims *by Margaret P. Pumphrey*   ISBN: *1-59462-116-0*   **$17.95**
This book explores pilgrims religious oppression in England as well as their escape to Holland and eventual crossing to America on the Mayflower, and their early days in New England...   History Pages 268

QTY

The Fasting Cure *by Sinclair Upton* ISBN: *1-59462-222-1* **$13.95**
In the Cosmopolitan Magazine for May, 1910, and in the Contemporary Review (London) for April, 1910, I published an article dealing with my experiences in fasting. I have written a great many magazine articles, but never one which attracted so much attention... New Age/Self Help/Health Pages 164

Hebrew Astrology *by Sepharial* ISBN: *1-59462-308-2* **$13.45**
In these days of advanced thinking it is a matter of common observation that we have left many of the old landmarks behind and that we are now pressing forward to greater heights and to a wider horizon than that which represented the mind-content of our progenitors... Astrology Pages 144

Thought Vibration or The Law of Attraction in the Thought World ISBN: *1-59462-127-6* **$12.95**
by William Walker Atkinson Psychology/Religion Pages 144

Optimism *by Helen Keller* ISBN: *1-59462-108-X* **$15.95**
Helen Keller was blind, deaf, and mute since 19 months old, yet famously learned how to overcome these handicaps, communicate with the world, and spread her lectures promoting optimism. An inspiring read for everyone... Biographies/Inspirational Pages 84

Sara Crewe *by Frances Burnett* ISBN: *1-59462-360-0* **$9.45**
In the first place, Miss Minchin lived in London. Her home was a large, dull, tall one, in a large, dull square, where all the houses were alike, and all the sparrows were alike, and where all the door-knockers made the same heavy sound... Childrens/Classic Pages 88

The Autobiography of Benjamin Franklin *by Benjamin Franklin* ISBN: *1-59462-135-7* **$24.95**
The Autobiography of Benjamin Franklin has probably been more extensively read than any other American historical work, and no other book of its kind has had such ups and downs of fortune. Franklin lived for many years in England, where he was agent... Biographies/History Pages 332

Name	
Email	
Telephone	
Address	
City, State ZIP	

☐ **Credit Card**   ☐ **Check / Money Order**

Credit Card Number	
Expiration Date	
Signature	

Please Mail to: Book Jungle
PO Box 2226
Champaign, IL 61825
or Fax to: 630-214-0564

ORDERING INFORMATION
web: *www.bookjungle.com*
email: *sales@bookjungle.com*
fax: *630-214-0564*
mail: *Book Jungle PO Box 2226 Champaign, IL 61825*
or PayPal *to sales@bookjungle.com*

Please contact us for bulk discounts

DIRECT-ORDER TERMS

20% Discount if You Order Two or More Books
Free Domestic Shipping!
Accepted: Master Card, Visa, Discover, American Express

www.ingramcontent.com/pod-product-compliance
Lightning Source LLC
LaVergne TN
LVHW081324060426
835511LV00011B/1846